ORIGAMI

The Diagram Group

BROCKHAMPTON
DIAGRAM
GUIDES

Origami

First published in Great Britain in 1997 by
Brockhampton Press Ltd
20 Bloomsbury Street
London
WC1 2QA
a member of the Hodder Headline Group PLC

ISBN 1-86019-812-0

Also in this series:
Boxing
Calligraphy
Card Games
Chinese Astrology
Drawing People
How the Body Works
Identifying Architecture
Kings and Queens of Britain
Magic Tricks
Party Games
Pub Games
SAS Survival Skills
Soccer Skills
Understanding Heraldry
World History

Introduction

Origami is the art of paper-folding. Originating in Japan many centuries ago, it has gradually spread to the West. As a pastime or hobby it has a universal appeal, whereby children and adults alike can feel the magic of creating something out of virtually nothing.

With a little time and patience you can easily acquire the skills needed to make the models in this book, including a butterfly, a swan and a fox. Few tools are needed, the material costs are small, and there is nothing to clean up when you finish.

This guide shows you how to make 10 models which are graded, ● Easy, ◆ Moderate, and ■ Difficult. They are laid out in this book with easy first, and difficult at the end, so you may progress your skills as you go.

First read the brief guidelines on page 6, then learn the symbols before going on to folding your first model. Always follow the simple step-by-step instructions, and study each complete folded model and the stages toward it, before you make your first fold.

Contents

Guidelines

- Use good, thick, strong paper. If available use 'origami' paper, which is usually coloured on one side, otherwise almost any paper will do.
- Makc sure your paper is cut square, whether you need to begin with a square or rectangular piece. You will have problems almost immediately if your paper is not cut accurately.
- Always fold or crease accurately. Careful and neat folding makes good models, careless folding can give you headaches. Use the back of your thumbnail to create firm creases or folds.
- Study each complete model and its stages of construction before you make your first fold.
- Familiarise yourself with the symbols below.
- Start with the easier models at the beginning of the book and progress to the more difficult models toward the end.

Tools

You will need a pencil and a ruler to measure and mark up the paper, and scissors to cut where required. Paper glue may be needed, although it is not essential.

Symbols

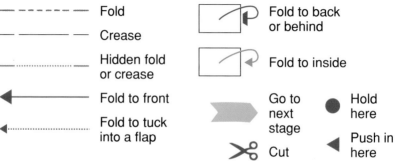

— — — — — —	Fold
— — — — —	Crease
—·······—	Hidden fold or crease
◄————	Fold to front
◄············	Fold to tuck into a flap

Fold to back or behind

Fold to inside

Go to next stage

Cut

Hold here

Push in here

● **Butterfly**

You will need
A square piece of paper,
about 20 cm x 20 cm, to
make a butterfly with a wing
span of approximately 20 cm.
Follow the seven easy stages
on these three pages.

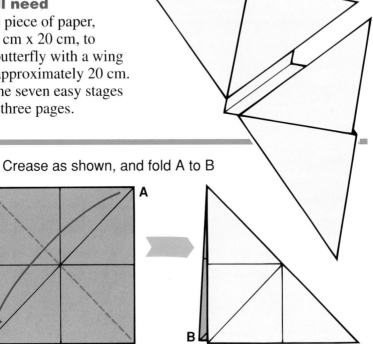

1 Crease as shown, and fold A to B

2 Fold A to C, pull D out to the
right and place E upon A

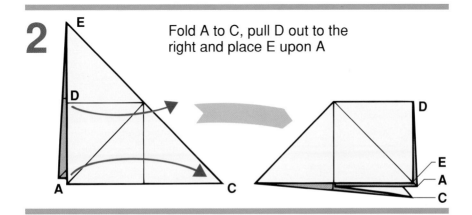

3   Fold E back to F, keeping A on C

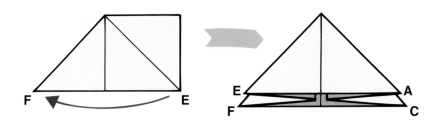

4   Turn up other way. Fold G to the front, so the
         point goes about 5 mm over edge AE

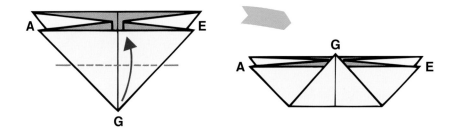

5   Fold flaps H and I down
         to the front

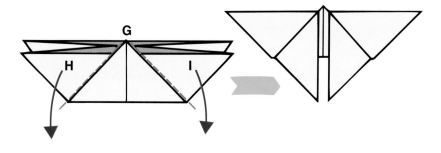

6

Fold in half to the
front, then open out
again

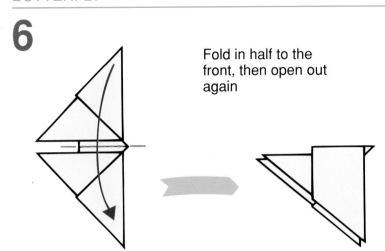

7

Make two folds, one on each side as shown (J,K),
fold back as in (**6**), and then fold each wing up in
turn, first L then M

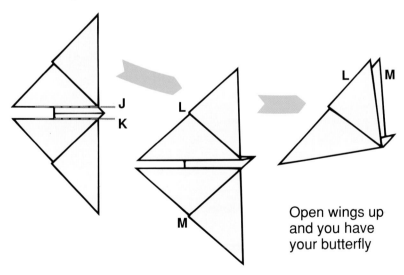

Open wings up
and you have
your butterfly

● Swan

You will need
A square piece of
paper 20 cm x 20 cm,
to make a swan about
10 cm high. Follow
the five easy stages
on these two pages.

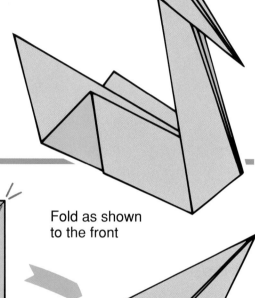

1

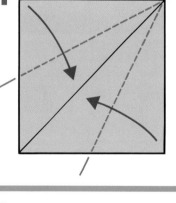

Fold as shown
to the front

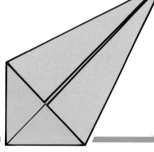

2

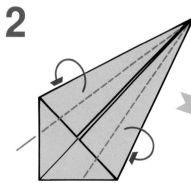

Fold as shown
to the back

3 Turn the paper over

Fold through the centre so A meets B

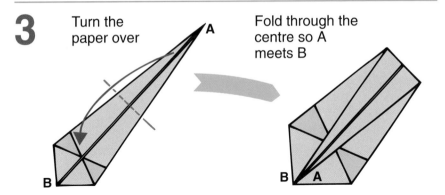

4

Fold A back 1/3 of the length

Fold in half lengthwise to the back

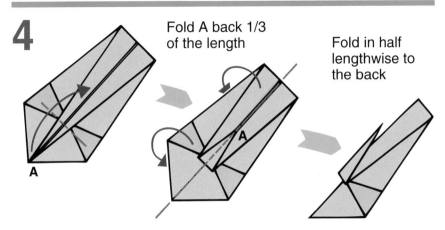

5 Hold at D and pull neck up at C

Make fold E and your swan is complete

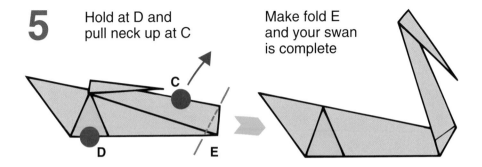

© DIAGRAM

● Hat

You will need
A rectangular piece of
paper, length one and a
half times its width. A
good size for a child is
40 cm x 60 cm. Paper
glue. Follow the five
easy stages on these
two pages.

1

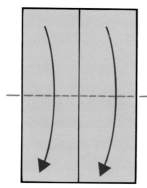

Crease along centre lengthwise
then fold in half as shown

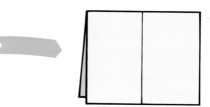

2 Fold corners A and B to the centre

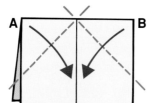

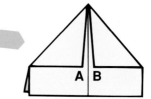

3 Fold front flap up as shown

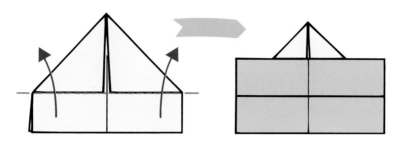

4 Turn over, and fold flap up as shown

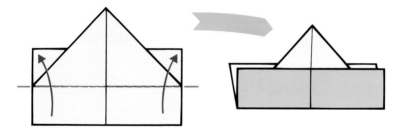

5 Glue the flaps together at C and D, then open out from the sides, and try it for size!

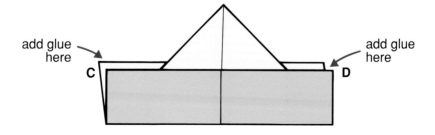

add glue here

add glue here

C

D

● Star

You will need
Two square pieces of paper, about 20 cm x 20 cm, to make a star about 12 cm high. Follow the eight easy stages on the next three pages.

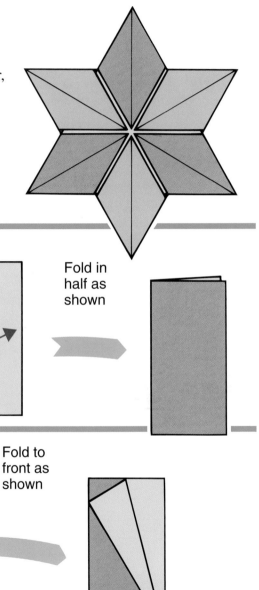

1

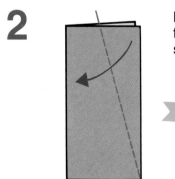

Fold in half as shown

2

Fold to front as shown

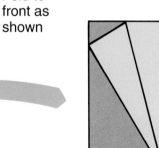

3 Cut along dotted line

Open out to form an
equilateral triangle

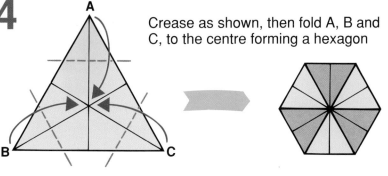

4

Crease as shown, then fold A, B and
C, to the centre forming a hexagon

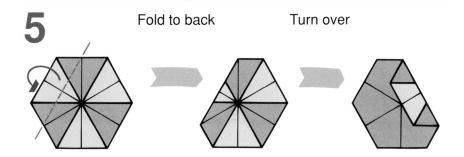

5 Fold to back   Turn over

6   Fold to front

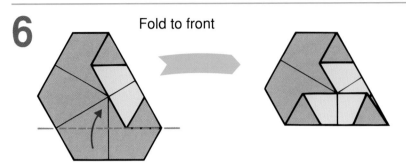

7   Fold to front and   Turn
          tuck D under E   over

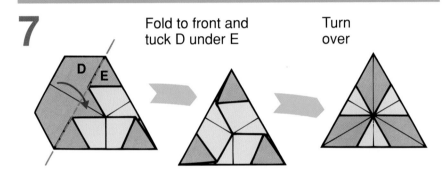

8   Repeat stages **1–7**
          to get a second
          triangle

Rotate one of them and slip it into
the other by lifting the flaps of the
lower triangle

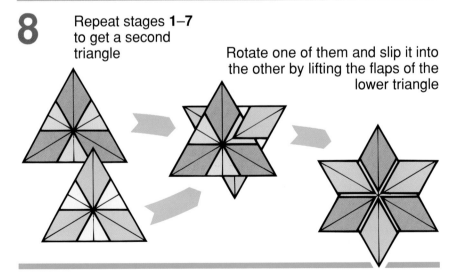

◆ Yacht

You will need
A square piece of
paper, about 20 cm
x 20 cm. This will
make a yacht about
20 cm long. Follow
the eight easy stages
on these next
four pages.

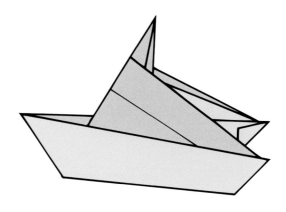

1

Make two creases as shown, then
fold corner A to the centre

2

Make a fold to the back as shown

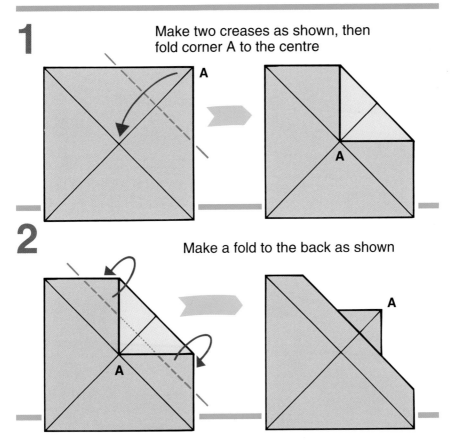

© DIAGRAM

3 Turn over, and make creases as shown. (BC is 2/5ths and CD is 3/5ths of the length of line BCD)

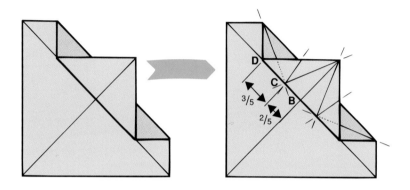

4 Fold along the creases as follows: points F fold forward and in to meet at point E, and points D fold upwards just short of edge G

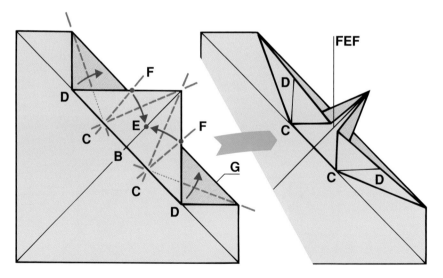

5

Turn over and make three creases as shown

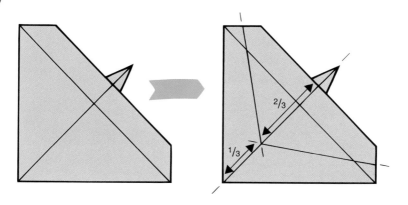

6

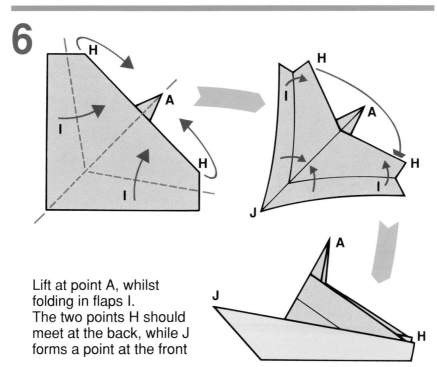

Lift at point A, whilst folding in flaps I.
The two points H should meet at the back, while J forms a point at the front

7 Fold front flap at the back of the boat to the inside as shown

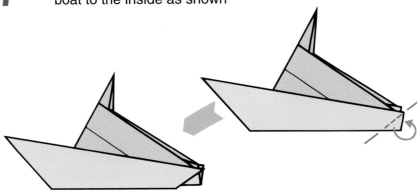

8 Do the same with the back flap. Fold it to the inside, and you have your finished yacht

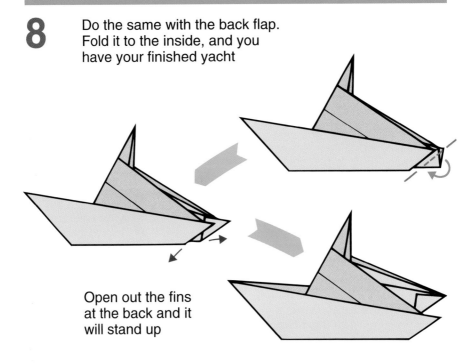

Open out the fins at the back and it will stand up

◆ Paper cube

You will need

A square piece of paper
about 20 cm x 20 cm will
make a cube with 5 cm-
long sides.
Follow the ten easy stages
on these four pages.

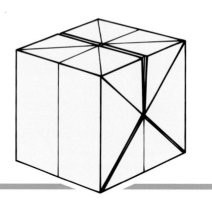

---

1 Crease as shown and fold A to B

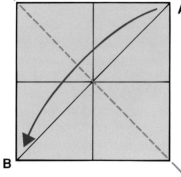

---

2 Fold A to C, pull D out to the
right and place E upon A

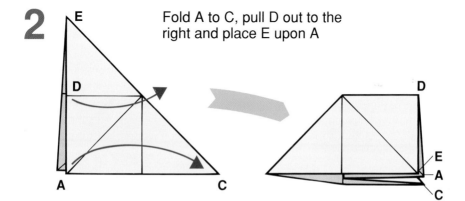

3   Fold E back to F, keeping A on C

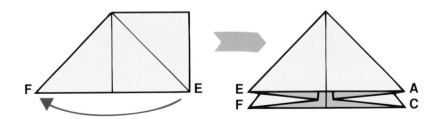

4   Turn up other way. Fold corners A and E to the
         front, to point G as shown

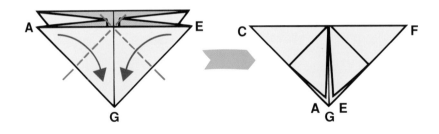

5   Turn over. Fold corners F and C to point G

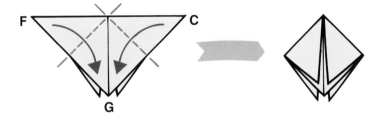

6 Fold as shown to the centre

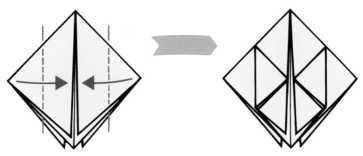

7 Turn over, and repeat the folds in (**6**) to the other side

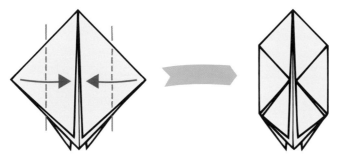

8 Fold lower flaps up and turn the paper over

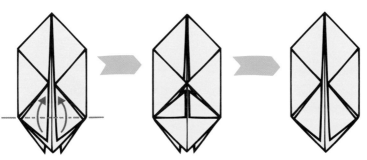

9

Repeat the folds of the lower flaps as in stage **8**

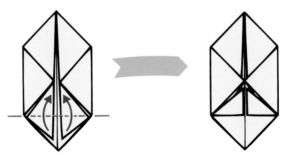

10

Fold and tuck inside the two small flaps so H meets J and I meets K. Then turn over and repeat the folds so L meets N and M meets O

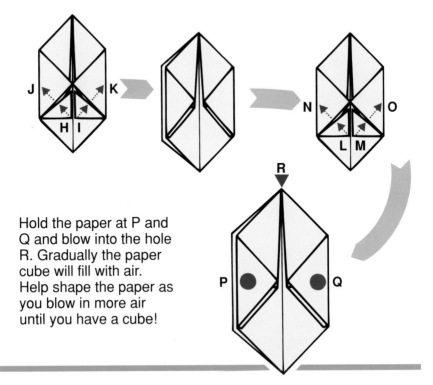

Hold the paper at P and Q and blow into the hole R. Gradually the paper cube will fill with air. Help shape the paper as you blow in more air until you have a cube!

◆ **Nodding dog**

You will need

Two pieces of square paper,
one for the body and one
for the head. Squares
20 cm x 20 cm will make
approximately a 14 cm-tall
dog. Follow the sixteen
stages on these seven pages.

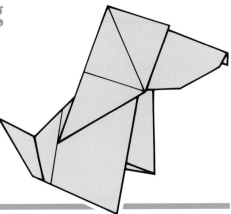

1

Crease and
fold as
shown

2

Make two further folds to
the front as shown

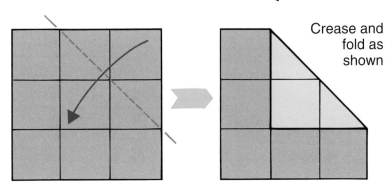

3 Make a fold to the back as shown, then turn over to other side

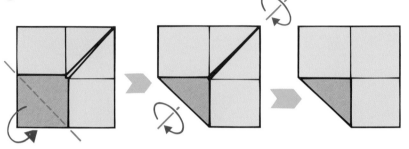

4 Make a fold as shown, then unfold it again to leave a crease

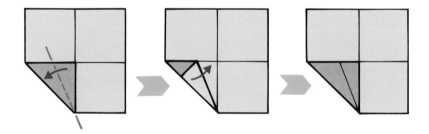

5 As above, make a further fold, then unfold it again to leave a crease

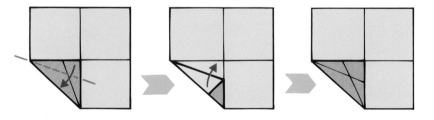

6

Make one last crease as shown (only in the top flap)

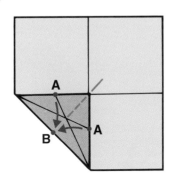

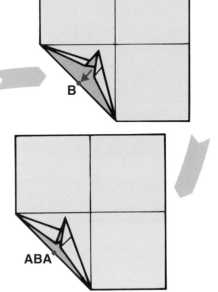

Then pull points
A together and
fold them down
to point B to
form what is
called a
'rabbit's ear'

7

Make two folds to the back as shown

8 Now fold in half along line C

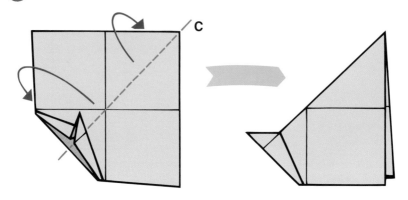

This is the completed body. Now for the head

9 Make the creases as shown here in the second sheet of paper. Then turn it over

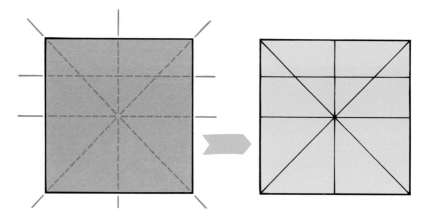

10 Make two folds to the front, unfold to leave creases, then turn the paper over

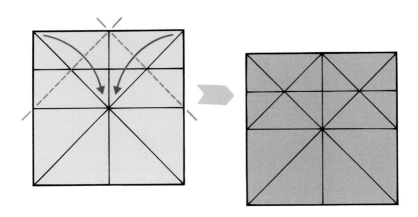

11 Make two folds to the centre as shown

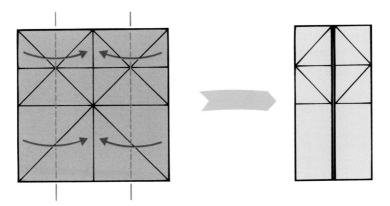

12

Fold along line C pulling points A toward imaginary points B

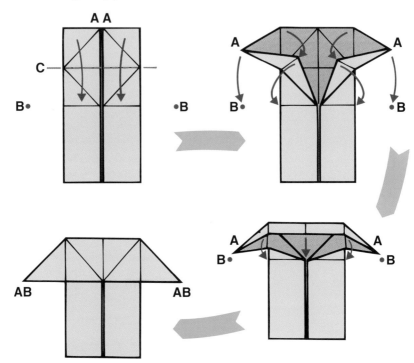

13

Fold in half to the back

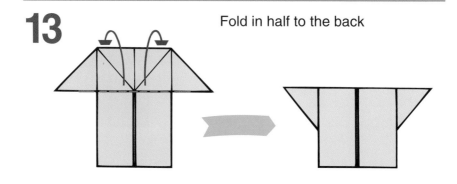

14 Fold the two flaps shown to the middle so corners D touch the centre line

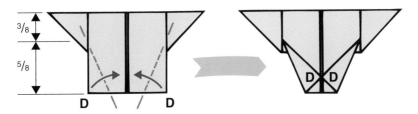

15 Make two further folds in the nose as shown

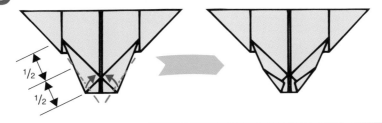

16 Turn as shown and fold in half. Hold in positions shown and pull nose down to create back of the head. Crease at E

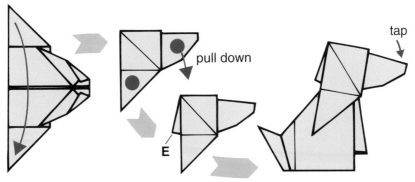

pull down

tap

Balance head on body, tap nose, and dog will nod!

■ Fox

You will need
A piece of paper of
length double its width;
15 cm x 30 cm will make
a fox about 14 cm tall.
Follow the ten stages
on the next five pages.

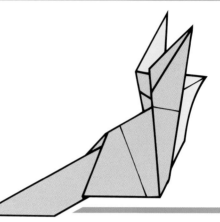

1 Make creases as shown and fold in the corners

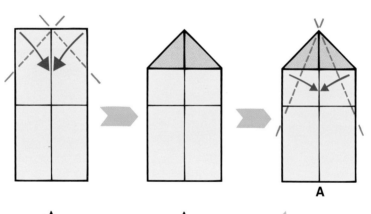

A

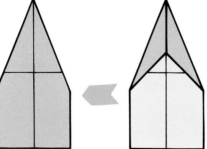

Fold in the two
flaps (above)
as shown to
centre line A.
Then turn the
paper over

2

Make creases and fold as shown. Then fold point A
to imaginary point B. Point C will rise up

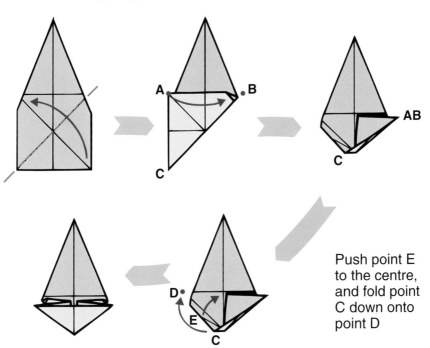

Push point E
to the centre,
and fold point
C down onto
point D

3

Make two creases as shown. Fold point F to point G
making point H rise up

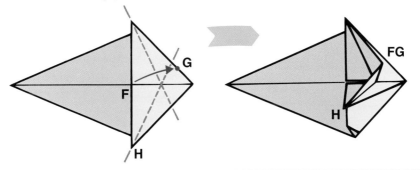

4

Now fold point H to point I

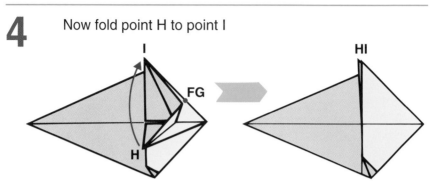

5

Fold in half along the centre leaving the pointed flaps H and I up

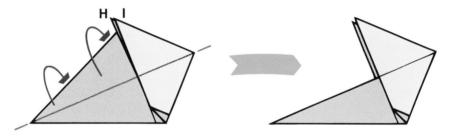

6

Make a fold as shown. Lift at J and pull tail down and to the inside of the body from point K

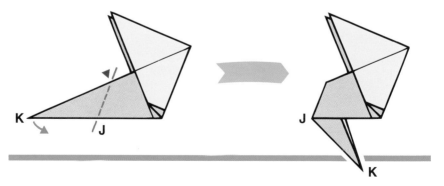

7

Make a fold so that edge L meets edge M

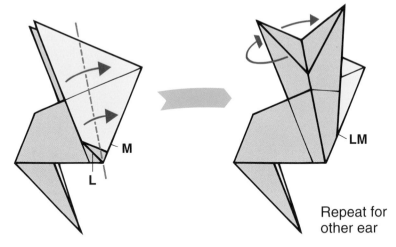

Repeat for
other ear

8

Make a fold in the tail flap as shown. Then lift front
flap at point N and bring tail up through inside of
body from point K

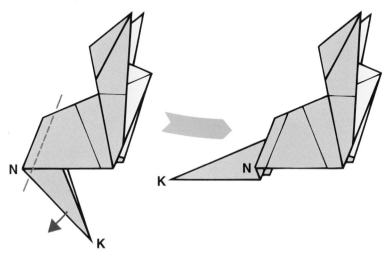

9

Make a fold at
the bottom
of the tail,
folding the
flap to the
inside of
the tail

Repeat the
fold on the
other side
of the tail

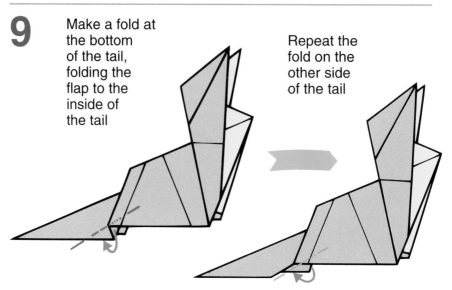

10

Now make a
curved fold on
each side of
the face, to
the inside

Open out a
little at P
and Q and
your fox will
stand up!

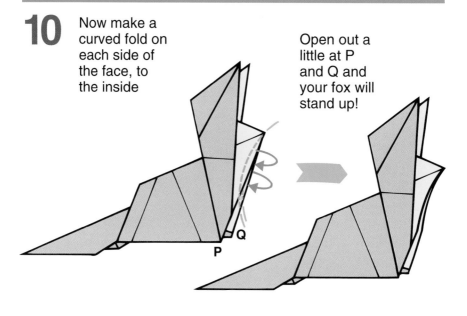

■ Fish

You will need
A square piece of paper,
30 cm x 30 cm to make
a fish 25 cm long.
Follow the twelve
stages on the next
five pages.

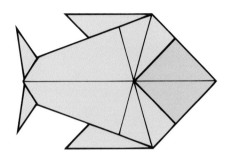

1 Make a crease diagonally along the centre. Then make two folds as shown to the centre, and unfold again

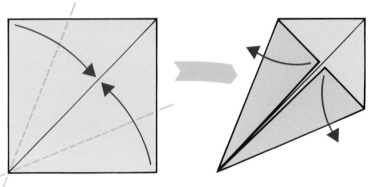

2 Make a fold to the front as shown

© DIAGRAM

3 Turn over and make two folds to the front

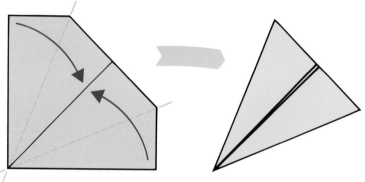

4 Make two folds to the centre, then unfold them leaving creases

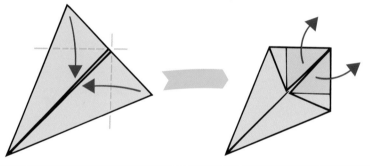

5 Fold A to B, then unfold leaving a crease

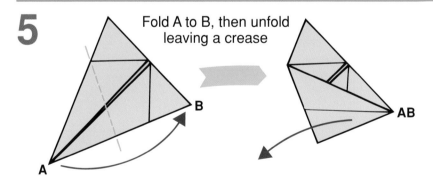

6

Fold A to C then unfold
leaving a crease

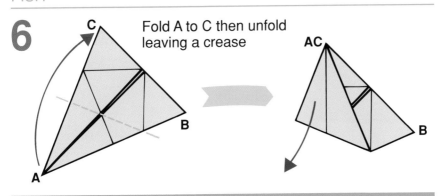

7

Pull points D down to imaginary points E. At the
same time push points B and C inward to centre

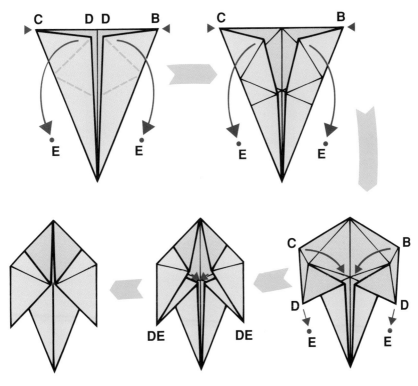

8 Make a fold in the tail as shown, then unfold it

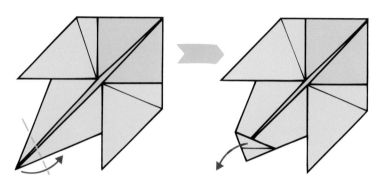

9 Make a second fold in the tail and again unfold it

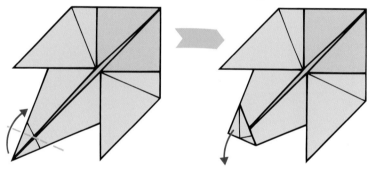

10 Cut along centre to point where the two creases intersect

11

Make fold F (parallel to fold G). Lift flap H at its point and pull it to the right and up, opening at I to form a kite shape

Fold kite shape in half to the left

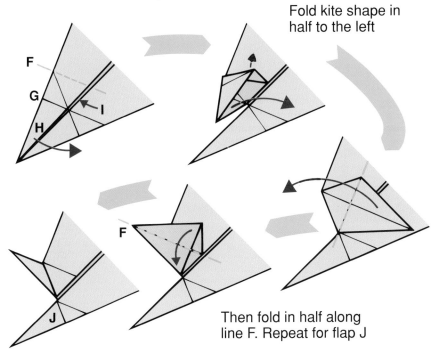

Then fold in half along line F. Repeat for flap J

12

Now turn it over for your finished fish!

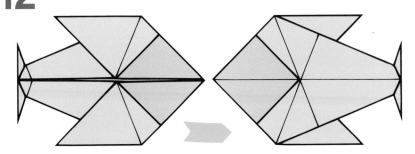

■ Resting bird

You will need
A square piece of paper,
30 cm x 30 cm, to make a
bird 30 cm long from head
to tail. Follow the nine
stages on the next
five pages.

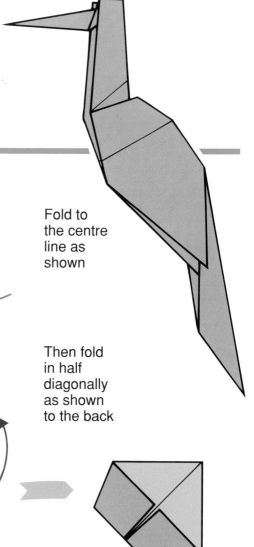

1

Fold to
the centre
line as
shown

Then fold
in half
diagonally
as shown
to the back

2

Pull points A down bringing
edges B to the centre

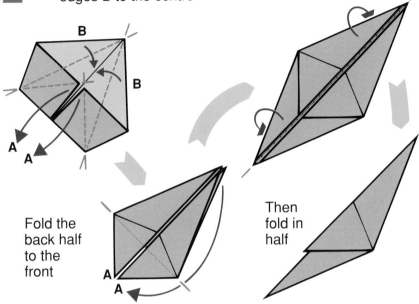

Fold the
back half
to the
front

Then
fold in
half

3

Hold as shown
and pull back
at point C

Then push at
the centre of
the kite shape
bringing points
D together

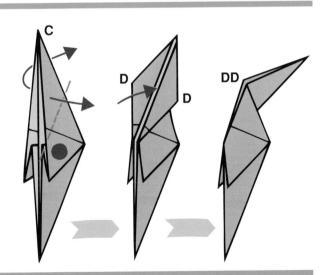

4 Make a folded crease as shown. Open the paper out slightly, and fold edges E round to the front to touch each other, pushing in at the centre F

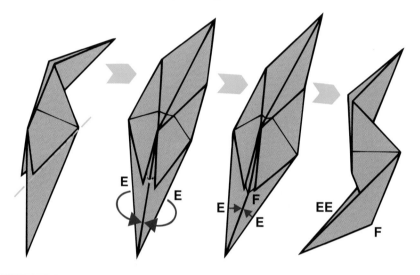

5 Make two creases in flap G as shown. Lift at H, and push point I under H, bringing edges J together. Repeat with other flap K

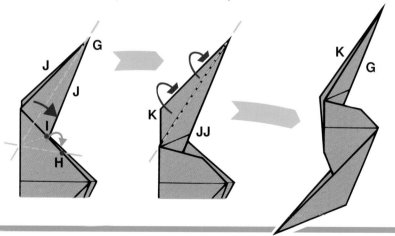

6

Make a folded crease as shown. Open the paper out slightly. Flaps L then fold to the back and point M comes out toward you. Then pull the flaps out on either side to create the wings N

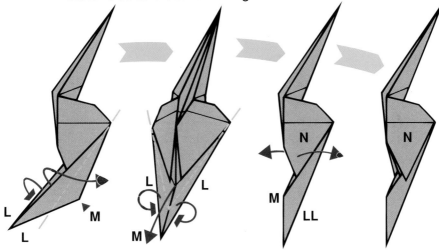

7

Make two folds in the edge of the bird's back as shown. Fold them to the inside so they are hidden. Repeat for the other side

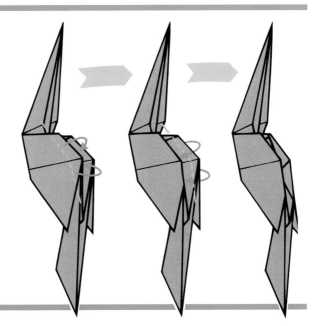

8

Fold front flap
back to form
kite shape.
Fold neck
down 1/3 of
its length to
the front

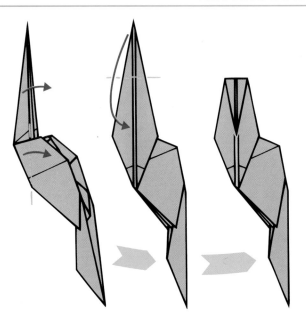

9

Make two further
creases in the
beak as shown.
Lift point O and
fold the flaps
back together

Pull slightly
on the beak
to open out
the face, and
your bird is
complete!

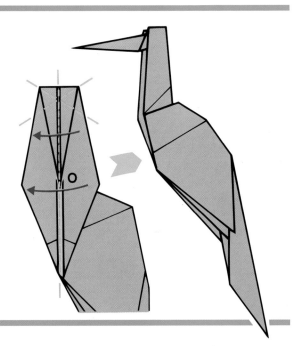